SOLAR POWER

NEIL MORRIS

Smart Apple Media

Published by Smart Apple Media
2140 Howard Drive West
North Mankato, MN 56003
Designed by Guy Callaby
Edited by Mary-Jane Wilkins
Artwork by Graham Rosewarne
Picture research by Su Alexander

Photographs by
Title page Reuters/Corbis; 4 Jeff Vanuga/Corbis; 5 Galen Rowell/Corbis; 7t NASA/Science Photo Library, b Jean-Pierre Lescourret/Corbis; 8 Archivo Iconografico, S.A./Corbis; 9 Alinari Archives/Corbis; 10 George D. Lepp/Corbis; 11 & 12 Chinch Gryniewicz; Ecoscene/Corbis; 13 Galen Rowell/Corbis; 14 Roger Ressmeyer/Corbis; 15 Paul Almasy/Corbis; 16 Reuters/Corbis; 17 Erik Schaffer; Ecoscene/Corbis; 18t Hashimoto Noboru/Corbis Sygma, b David Hancock/Reuters/Corbis; 19 Reuters/Corbis; 20 NASA/Corbis Sygma; 21t Reuters/Corbis, b Fred Prouser/Reuters/Corbis; 22 Michael S. Yamashita/ Corbis; 23 Gideon Mendel/Corbis; 24 Ted Soqui/Corbis; 25t Paul A. Souders/ Corbis, b Martin B. Withers; Frank Lane Picture Agency/Corbis; 26 Roger Ressmeyer/Corbis; 27 Dorothy Burrows; Eye Ubiquitous/Corbis; 28 Corbis; 29 G. Rossenbach/ZEFA; Front cover: Otto Rogge/Corbis

Printed in China

Library of Congress Cataloging-in-Publication Data

Morris, Neil, 1946-
Solar power / by Neil Morris.
p. cm. – (Energy sources)
Includes index.
ISBN-13: 987-1-58340-908-4
1. Solar energy–Juvenile literature. I. Title. II. Series.

TJ810.3.M67 2006
333.792'3–dc22 2006042238

First Edition

9 8 7 6 5 4 3 2 1

Contents

Power from the sun

The word "solar" comes from the Latin word for sun, which is the most powerful energy source we know. The sun's rays travel through space to our planet and provide us with light and heat.

On a bright, sunny day, we can both see and feel the sun's energy. We can also collect and use solar power to work machines, as well as to light and heat our homes, offices, and factories, even when it is cold and dark outside.

The term "energy" comes from the Greek word *energos*, meaning active or working. Energy sources help other things become active and do work, such as lifting or moving objects. For example, solar power can be used to make electricity. So when you switch on a solar-powered light or calculator, the energy to make it work comes directly from the power of the sun.

The sun rises every day. Its energy makes life on Earth possible.

Wind and water

We live on a solar-powered planet. The sun is our ultimate energy source because it drives other sources, such as wind and water. The sun's rays warm some parts of the world more than others, and this affects the blanket of air that surrounds our planet. It creates the movement of air that we call wind. At the same time, solar energy heats the world's oceans, creating clouds and rain in a never-ending water cycle. It also made the world's fossil fuels—coal, oil, and natural gas—which come from the fossilized remains of prehistoric plants and animals. They could never have existed without the sun.

Capturing sunlight

The world's plants rely on solar power. They capture sunlight and use it to combine carbon dioxide from the air and water from soil. This combining process, called photosynthesis, helps plants make their own sugary food. At the same time, they give off oxygen, which other living things—including humans—need to breathe and stay alive. When animals eat plants, they are nourished by the plants' food. Solar power is essential to Earth's food cycle.

RENEWABLE RESOURCE

Solar power is a renewable resource because it is not in danger of running out. Some other energy sources, such as coal and oil, are burned and used up to produce power. Geothermal, water, wind, and biomass power are also renewable forms of energy.

A tree's leaves act like solar panels. They use a green chemical called chlorophyll to absorb sunlight.

Our own star

The sun is a star—a giant, hot ball of burning gases that gives off heat and shines with its own light. It does this by a process called nuclear fusion, in which the central parts of atoms (called nuclei) fuse (join together) to form the nuclei of other atoms.

At the center of the sun, in its core, an enormously high temperature of 27 million °F (15 million °C) causes the nuclei of atoms of hydrogen gas to change. They fuse to form the nucleus of helium atoms and at the same time give off enormous amounts of energy. The energy flows up to the surface of the sun and then travels out into space in all directions. Only a small fraction of this energy reaches Earth, which is tiny compared with its star. The sun's volume is more than a million times greater than Earth's.

photosphere
convection zone
radiative zone
core

A cutaway of the sun. The temperature of its surface layer, called the photosphere, is much lower than at the core. But it's still a very hot 9,900 °F (5,500 °C)!

Light and heat rays

The sun gives off most of its energy in the form of electrical and magnetic waves. The range of this electromagnetic radiation includes infrared waves, which we feel as heat, and visible light rays. Radio waves and x-rays are also in the range.

All of these rays and waves travel through space at the speed of light. At nearly186,000 miles (300,000 km) per second, this is the fastest speed in the universe. The sun's energy shoots through 93.2 million miles (150 million km) of space and reaches Earth in just over 8 minutes.

Radiation sometimes bursts out of the sun's photosphere in a solar flare.

The seasons

The amount of solar radiation—which we usually call sunshine—varies at any particular spot on Earth according to the season. Summer is warmer than winter, and there are more hours of sunshine during the summer.

The seasons happen because Earth spins on an axis that is tilted instead of being straight. So when the northern half of the planet is tilted toward the sun, the solar rays are more intense, and it is summer there. Near the equator, temperatures remain much the same year-round. The seasons have an effect on how we use solar energy.

A summery scene in a London park. In midsummer, the temperature averages 64 °F (18 °C). In midwinter, it is just 39 °F (4 °C).

Knowledge and beliefs

People have known about the power of the sun from the earliest times. In ancient Greece, great teachers advised people to build their homes facing south. Philosophers such as Socrates and Aristotle taught that houses should be built so that they could be heated by the sun.

In parts of ancient Greece and Asia Minor, whole cities were laid out in a pattern that gave all homes plenty of sunlight in both the summer and the winter. The Romans carried on this tradition. By the first century A.D., they added glass to window openings so that rooms acted as solar heat traps. This later led to the introduction of glass-covered roofs, which became popular in northern Europe beginning in the 16th century. All of these methods are known as passive solar heating —they allow the sun to light and heat buildings in the best way.

In this ancient Egyptian sculpture, the pharaoh Akhenaten (whose name meant "glory of the sun disk") bathes in the rays of the sun god Aten.

Gods, myths, and legends

Many ancient civilizations worshipped the sun as the great force of life. The Egyptian god Aten took the form of the sun disk, and around 1350 B.C., the pharaoh worshipped him as the only god. In ancient Greek mythology, the sun god Helios was the brother of Selene (the moon) and Eos (the dawn). Helios drove his chariot across the sky every day and floated back across the ocean at night in a golden cup.

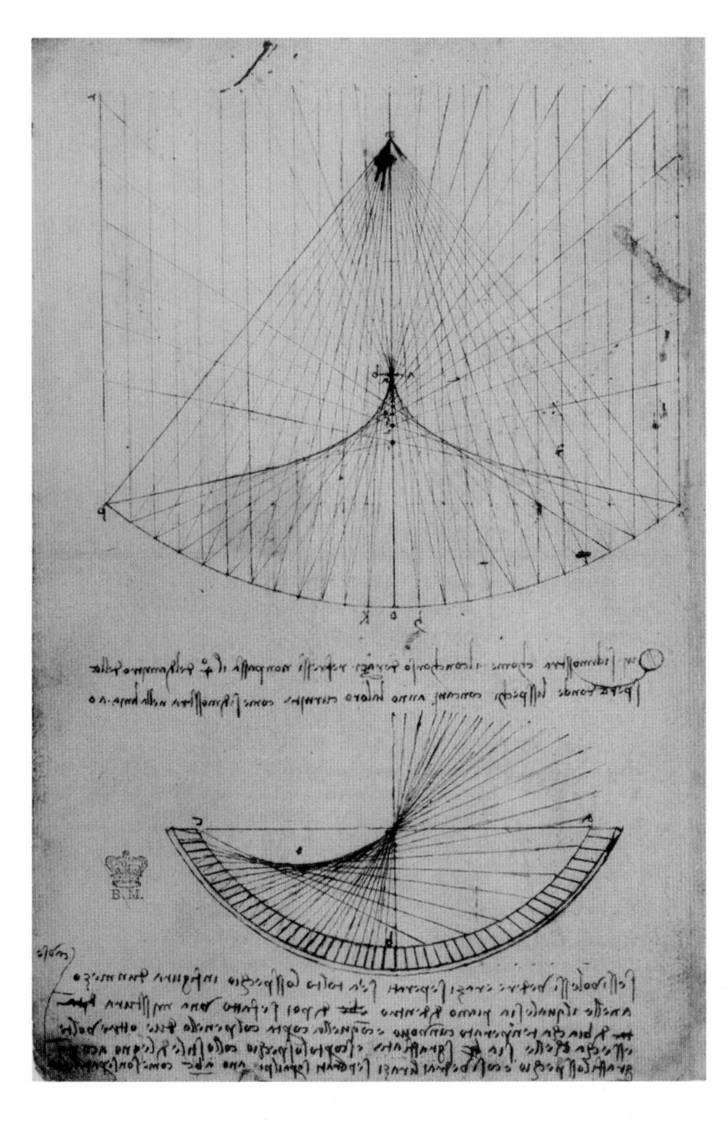

Scientific discoveries

In 1515, Italian artist and scientist Leonardo da Vinci drew designs for a large, curved mirror. The plan was for the mirror to concentrate the sun's rays onto a boiler and heat water for dyeing cloth.

In 1770, French chemist Antoine Lavoisier used joined pieces of glass filled with wine in a similar way to melt the metal platinum. Sixty-nine years later, another French scientist—Edmond Becquerel—discovered that electricity passed between two metal plates when one was exposed to sunlight. This eventually led to the invention of the solar cell (see page 10).

This drawing by Leonardo da Vinci shows how a mirror reflects the sun's rays.

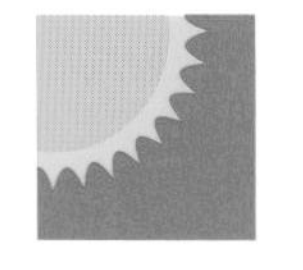

Solar cells

Have you ever seen a solar-powered pocket calculator or wristwatch? If so, you might have wondered how solar power works. The answer is that the watch and calculator run on solar cells.

A solar cell is a small device that produces electricity directly from sunlight. It is also called a photovoltaic (PV) cell (from photo, meaning light, and volt, a unit of electrical force). Solar cells were first made in the 19th century, and they have become much more powerful in recent years.

Today, some cells can convert up to a quarter of the sunlight that shines on them into electricity. They are usually very small, which is useful for calculators and watches, but this means that they produce

A close-up of photovoltaic cells on a solar panel.

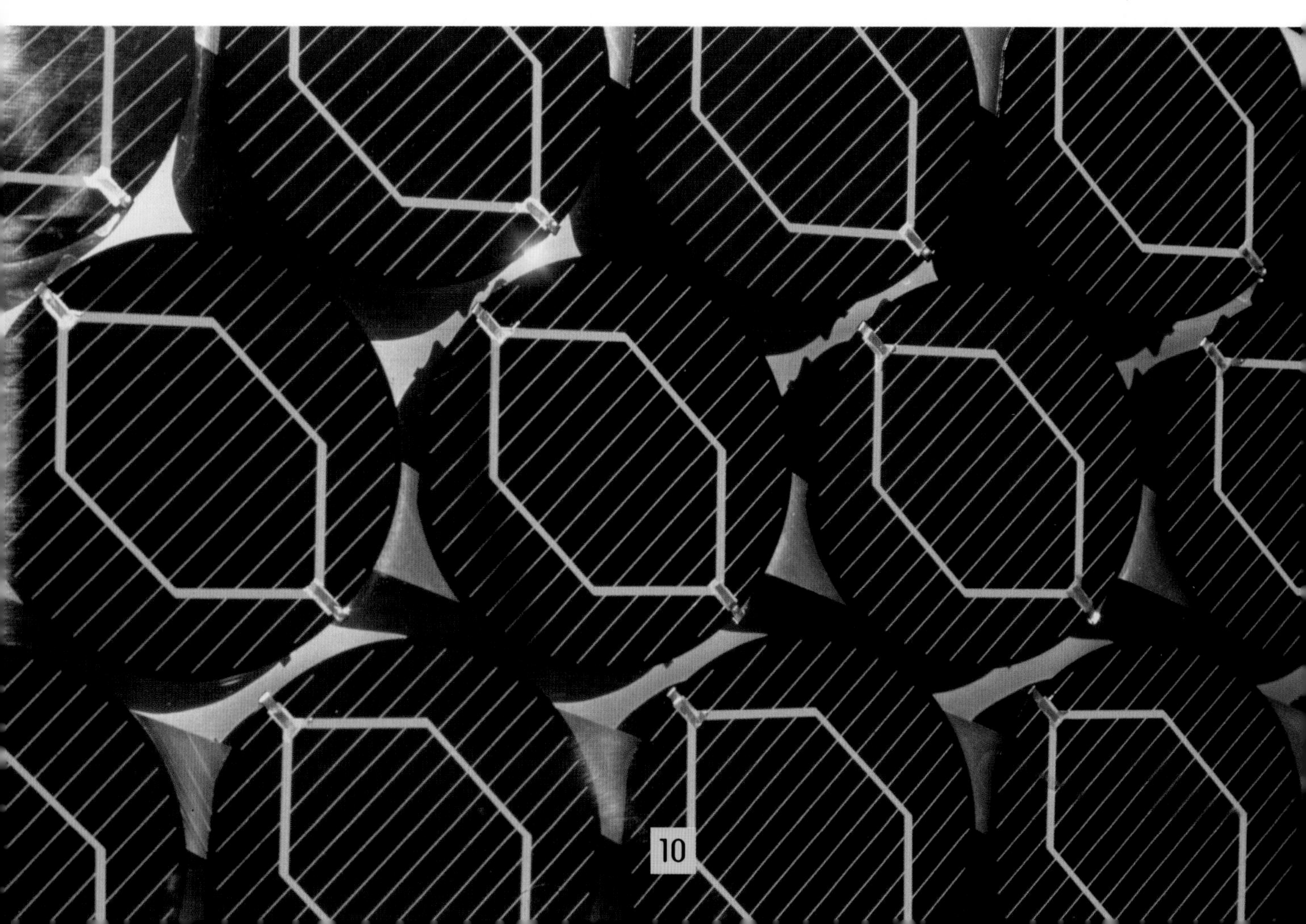

a fairly weak electric current. For larger use and more power, solar cells are put together in rows on a panel, which can be turned to face the sun.

Flowing particles

PV cells work by the movement of electrons, which are particles that occur in atoms. Sunlight passes through the glass cover of the cell and hits atoms in two separate layers of the chemical element silicon. One is an n (for negative) layer, and the other is positive. When the light hits the junction between the two layers, the p-layer loses electrons, and the n-layer collects them. This causes electrons to pass between the metal contacts at the front and back of the cell, creating a flow of electricity.

STORING LIGHT

One of the best and most common uses of solar cells is for lighting. People buy solar lamps for their garden and many other outdoor places. During the day, PV cells on top of a lamp convert sunlight into electricity, which is stored in a rechargeable battery. When it grows dark, the battery operates a bulb to turn the electricity back into light. Solar lamps are not usually as powerful or bright as some other kinds, but they cost nothing to run.

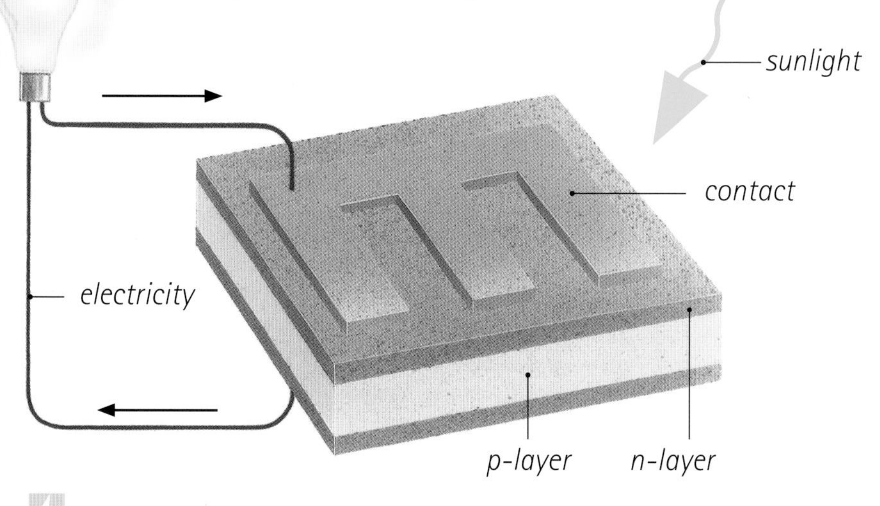

This diagram shows the parts of a PV cell. The two layers are made of silicon, which is an element found in sand and various minerals.

When Mumbles lighthouse, in Wales, was built in 1794, its light came from two burning coal fires. These were later changed to oil lamps, and since 1995, the electric lamp has been powered by solar panels.

Heat panels

Solar power is often used for heating homes and swimming pools. One way to do this is to install solar cells and then use electricity to run the heating system. But there is an easier way, using flat-plate (or flat-bed) collectors.

These collectors are made up of a shallow metal box with a glass cover on top and a dark-colored plate at the bottom. The glass traps heat, and the plate absorbs it. Water (or sometimes another liquid) is pumped slowly through thin pipes attached to the absorber plate. The water takes in heat energy from sunshine and becomes hot.

The hot water then flows to a device called a heat exchanger, which transfers the heat to the hot-water supply for the house or swimming pool. The collector panels are usually placed on the roof of a building.

This small collector panel heats the water for a house in Lanzarote, one of the Canary Islands.

This man is boiling water over a simple solar cooker.

Trapping heat

Gardeners use greenhouses as a form of solar heating for delicate plants. They are made of glass, or sometimes plastic, on a thin metal or wooden frame. Just like a solar collector, the glass roof and walls let in sunlight and then trap it inside the greenhouse. A small amount of heat passes back through the glass, but very slowly.

Solar cooking

Light, shiny surfaces have a different effect on the sun's rays. They reflect sunlight rather than absorbing it. This is how Leonardo da Vinci's solar-heating mirror worked (see page 9). The same system is used in some parts of the world for boiling water and cooking food. Curved pieces of shiny metal reflect sunlight onto a small area, where a metal ring can hold a pot or kettle. This simple piece of equipment is very effective and can easily be turned and tipped up or down to face the sun at different times of the day.

THE GREENHOUSE EFFECT

Earth's atmosphere acts in the same way as the glass walls and roof of a greenhouse, keeping the planet warm by trapping heat. This is called the greenhouse effect. It is natural, but polluting gases have added to the effect.

Power plants

The sun's energy can be used to produce electricity in power plants. These plants use a different system from solar cells. They work in a similar way to solar collectors, but they concentrate and increase the power of heat rays by reflecting them onto a spot.

In one system used in the Mojave Desert of California, long rows of curved reflectors face the sun. They bounce sunlight onto thin steel pipes and heat the fluid inside to 750 °F (400 °C). In another part of the plant, this heat is used to make steam. The steam turns the blades of a turbine, as in other kinds of power stations, such as coal-fired or nuclear plants. The turbine

Rows of curved reflecting troughs at a solar power plant in California.

is attached to a generator that produces electricity. Other solar systems have hundreds of movable mirrors, called heliostats, which reflect sunlight onto a central tower. This concentrates the solar power up to 1,500 times.

Solar furnace

Another kind of power plant, called a solar furnace, uses a set of small heliostats to reflect sunlight onto a large, curved mirror. The sunlight then bounces off the mirror and is focused onto a central tower, where fluid can be heated. This double reflection system creates temperatures of up to 5,400 °F (3,000 °C). There is a solar furnace at Odeillo, in the French Pyrenees mountains. This has 63 heliostats, each 20 feet (6 m) tall, which reflect onto a silver-backed glass mirror that is made up of 9,130 square reflectors.

This photograph shows the large, curved mirror at Odeillo, in France. The mirror is 130 feet (40 m) high. You can see the central tower on the right.

Solar tower

The solar tower, sometimes called a solar chimney, is a new development. A test tower has worked in Spain, and there are plans to build the real thing in Australia. Planners say that the Australian concrete tower will be 3,250 feet (990 m) tall—much higher than the world's tallest building. It will be surrounded on the ground by a huge circular greenhouse, where the sun's rays will heat the air. Since hot air rises, it will rush up the tower at more than 30 miles (50 km) per hour. The moving air will turn wind turbines, which will be attached to electric generators. Cooler air will enter the greenhouse at the sides.

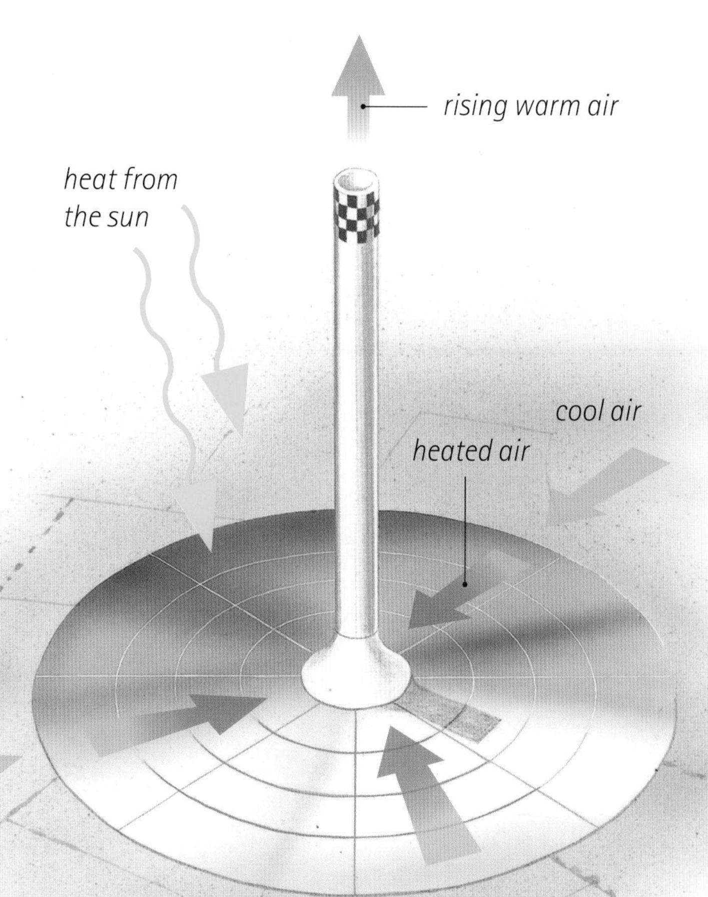

An artist's impression of a solar tower. Scientists say it will generate enough electricity for 200,000 homes.

Small-scale use

By the 1960s, scientists had developed solar cells that produced useful amounts of electricity. They were used to power all sorts of devices, especially items that needed to be lightweight and could be carried around.

Some devices used rechargeable batteries, and others had other types of batteries for back-up. This meant that if there was a lot of sunshine, the radio, calculator, or lamp worked on solar power. But if it was dark or cloudy, you could switch over to an ordinary battery.

This led to solar cells powering larger machines such as refrigerators. In recent years, the cells have become more efficient, and as more have been sold, they have become cheaper, too.

This robot jellyfish was made by a Japanese toy company. Called an aquaroid, it is propelled by a solar cell as it swims in a water tank.

This house in southern Spain lies across the valley from the nearest village and uses solar cells to produce its own electricity.

ECO-FRIENDLY POWER

Solar power is very practical and is particularly useful for people who do not get electricity from a national grid. Environmentalists say that it is "clean and green," or eco-friendly, because solar production and use do not harm the environment or pollute our planet. Small-scale use of solar power allows people to be independent of huge energy companies. They can connect their solar system to a battery that stores the electricity generated and acts as the main power supply for their home.

Gadgets and toys

Many companies use solar technology to power the gadgets they sell. These include sensors, switches, phones, flashlights, and even power tools. Most use PV cells with rechargeable batteries, and there are even solar-powered battery chargers. Solar power is popular with toy manufacturers, too, and some robot toys operate by solar cells. This use of solar technology may seem to be just for fun, but it might lead to more serious developments in the future.

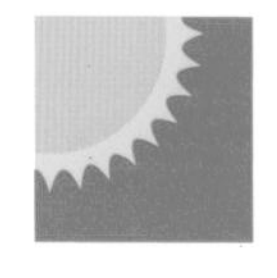

On the move

Great advances have been made recently in using the sun's energy to power vehicles. Scientists, engineers, and inventors have adapted solar power to transportation.

Many of the developments have come about because of challenges and races. Some of the vehicles are not intended for everyday use, but they show potential for the future. In 1981, American inventor Paul MacCready flew his *Solar Challenger* aircraft 175 miles (280 km) from France to England, reaching a height of 10,825 feet (3,300 m). The aircraft had more than 16,000 solar cells mounted on its wings. Seventeen years later, an American remote-controlled solar plane called *Pathfinder* set an altitude record of more than 78,740 feet (24,000 m). The first solar cars were driven in the 1980s, and they were soon joined by solar boats.

In 1996, Japanese sailor Kenichi Horie crossed the Pacific Ocean from Ecuador to Japan in this boat. Its solar panels drove the boat's engine.

This Taiwanese solar car completed the World Solar Challenge in less than 62 hours. Formosun II *came in 13th in the 2003 race.*

World Solar Challenge

In 1982, Hans Tholstrup drove his solar-powered car *Quiet Achiever* across Australia from Perth to Sydney. It took him 20 days and inspired the Australian inventor to start a challenge race, which is usually run every two years. Solar cars from all over the world drive more than 1,865 miles (3,000 km) across the Australian desert from Darwin to Adelaide. The first World Solar Challenge was held in 1987, with a field of 23 solar-powered cars. In September 2005, a Dutch car took less than 30 hours on the road to win the race, at an average speed of 64 miles (103 km) per hour.

Flying wing

In 2001, an experimental UAV (uninhabited aerial vehicle, or remote-controlled aircraft) from the United States set a world record by reaching a height of 96,864 feet (29,524 m). The aircraft, called *Helios* after the Greek sun god, was really a flying wing. Its 14 propellers were powered by 62,120 solar cells spread across the top of the wing, which was 245 feet (75 m) wide. Two years later, it crashed into the Pacific Ocean after taking off from Hawaii.

The Helios *pilotless aircraft on a test flight in 2001.*

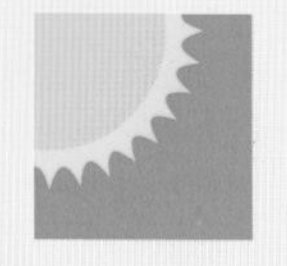

Space travel

Solar cells can be even more effective in the emptiness of space, where there are no clouds or seasons, than they are on Earth. Because of this, solar cells have played an important part in the history of space travel.

Round and drum-shaped satellites turn as they orbit Earth, so they have solar cells all the way around them. They need electricity to operate their computers, cameras, and radio links. When a solar-powered satellite is on the dark side of Earth, hidden from the sun, it uses batteries. Larger craft, including space stations and the Hubble Space Telescope, have flat panels. These stick out like wings and can turn to face the sun at the best angle. In recent years, solar cells have even powered robotic vehicles on the planet that is next farthest from the sun—Mars.

Space-shuttle astronauts work on an Intelsat communications satellite. Its outer shell is covered with solar cells.

International Space Station

The first part of the International Space Station was launched in 1998. New modules have been added during 40 missions to the station, which is supported by a partnership of 16 different countries. The station orbits Earth at a height of about 260 miles (420 km), and is powered by a large array of solar panels mounted on a metal framework. Each of the

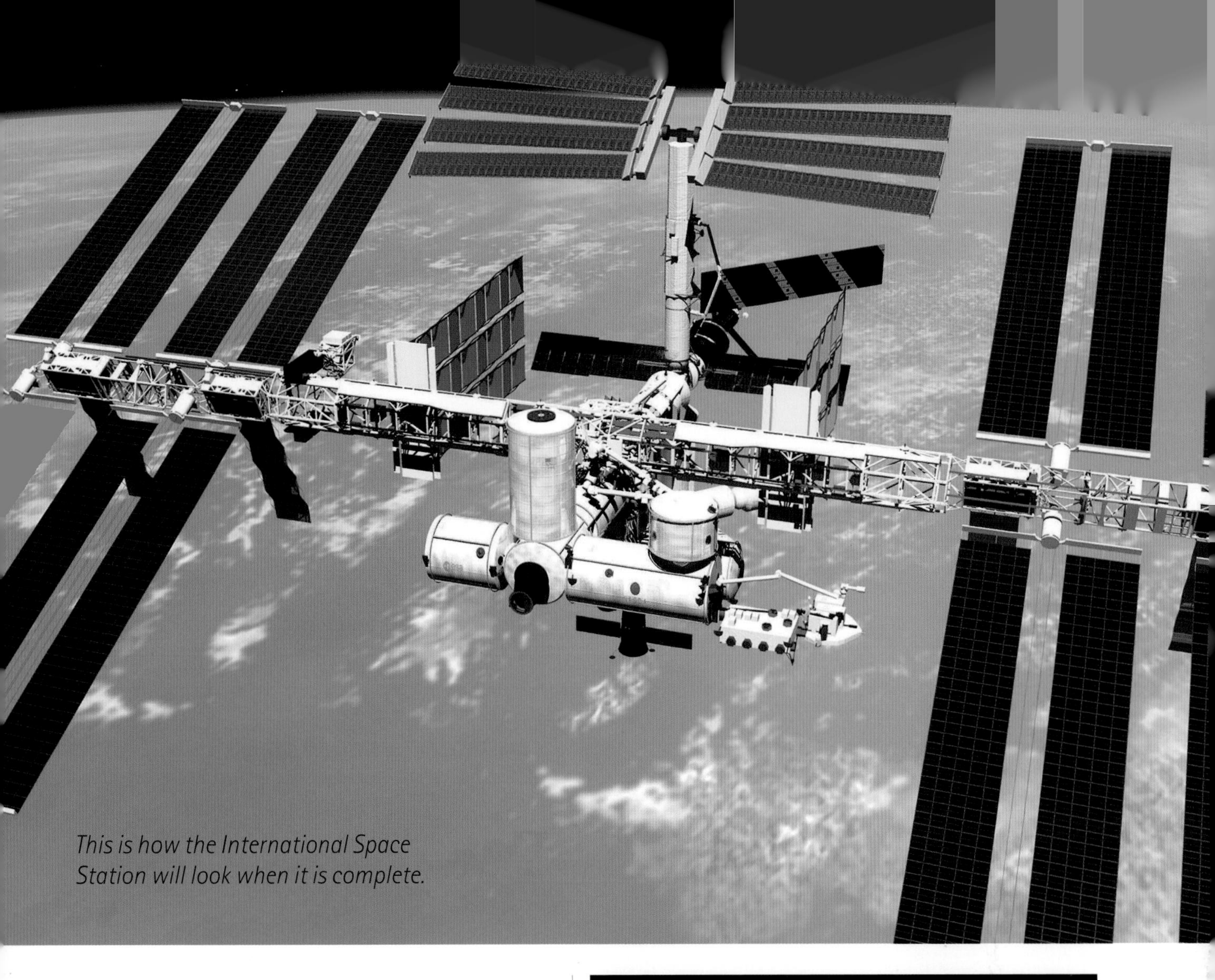

This is how the International Space Station will look when it is complete.

solar wings is 108 feet (33 m) long, and together they provide much more power than any earlier solar spacecraft.

Rover probes

In January 2004, two spacecraft landed on Mars, bounced on the surface, and then opened up to reveal exploration rovers. Called *Spirit* and *Opportunity*, the two rovers were soon moving across the planet, sending amazing photographs back to Earth. They are powered by flat solar panels and rechargeable batteries. Mars is many millions of miles farther away from the sun than Earth is, and the rovers were sent to a region near the Martian equator so that they could get enough sunlight.

A model of exploration rover Spirit, *showing its flat, brown wings of solar cells.*

Around the world

The sun shines all over the world and can be used everywhere as an energy source. Earth's sunnier regions are warmer, but solar technology works well in the cold polar regions, too.

Solar cells are used to power scientific bases in Antarctica, as well as small communities in the Arctic region of northern Canada. Special containers protect the batteries from extremely low temperatures.

At the beginning of the 21st century, nearly half of the world's PV power is produced in Asia. Japan is the world's leading PV producer, followed by the U.S. Europe produces a quarter of the planet's solar power, and Germany is the leading country. This energy source is becoming more important on all of the world's continents, especially in those countries where communities are not provided with electricity from a national grid.

A television broadcasting center is lit up at night in Tokyo. Japan leads the world in the production of solar-cell power, but solar power represents a tiny fraction of all the electricity the country uses.

Solar power in India

India is Asia's second-largest producer of electricity from solar cells, after Japan. Much of this power has been used to supply fresh drinking water to villages that do not have electric lines. Solar-powered pumps also help farmers water their fields and cattle, so they are able to use much less diesel oil and other fossil fuels.

Many people in small Indian communities use solar ovens. In 1999, the world's largest solar cooking system was set up in the desert region of Rajasthan. This system can prepare food for 10,000 people and is backed up by oil-fired boilers for the rare times when there is not enough sunshine.

European development

The countries of the European Union use more electricity than any single country, apart from the U.S. Germany is the biggest European consumer, as well as the largest user of solar power. Other European countries, led by Italy and Switzerland, are trying to use more of the sun's energy. In the UK and many other countries, homeowners are offered grants to help install solar panels on their roofs. In Spain, a law introduced in 2004 requires all new and renovated buildings to be fitted with solar panels.

Solar panels help to heat this house in a Scottish eco-village, where people rely on solar and wind power for their energy.

Renewable benefits

Scientists believe that the sun will continue to warm Earth for another 5 billion years and that there is little danger of its power weakening much before then.

This gives renewable energy from solar power an enormous advantage over nonrenewable energy sources such as fossil fuels. We know that our planet's coal, oil, and gas are gradually running out. Experts predict that reserves of coal will last little longer than 200 years, while oil and gas may run out in about 60 years' time. Yet most of today's electricity is produced by power stations burning fossil fuels. So it makes sense for us to try to increase our use of renewable resources such as wind, water, solar, and biomass power.

This new building in Los Angeles, California, has nearly 900 solar panels built into its windows. The PV panels help produce electricity for the building.

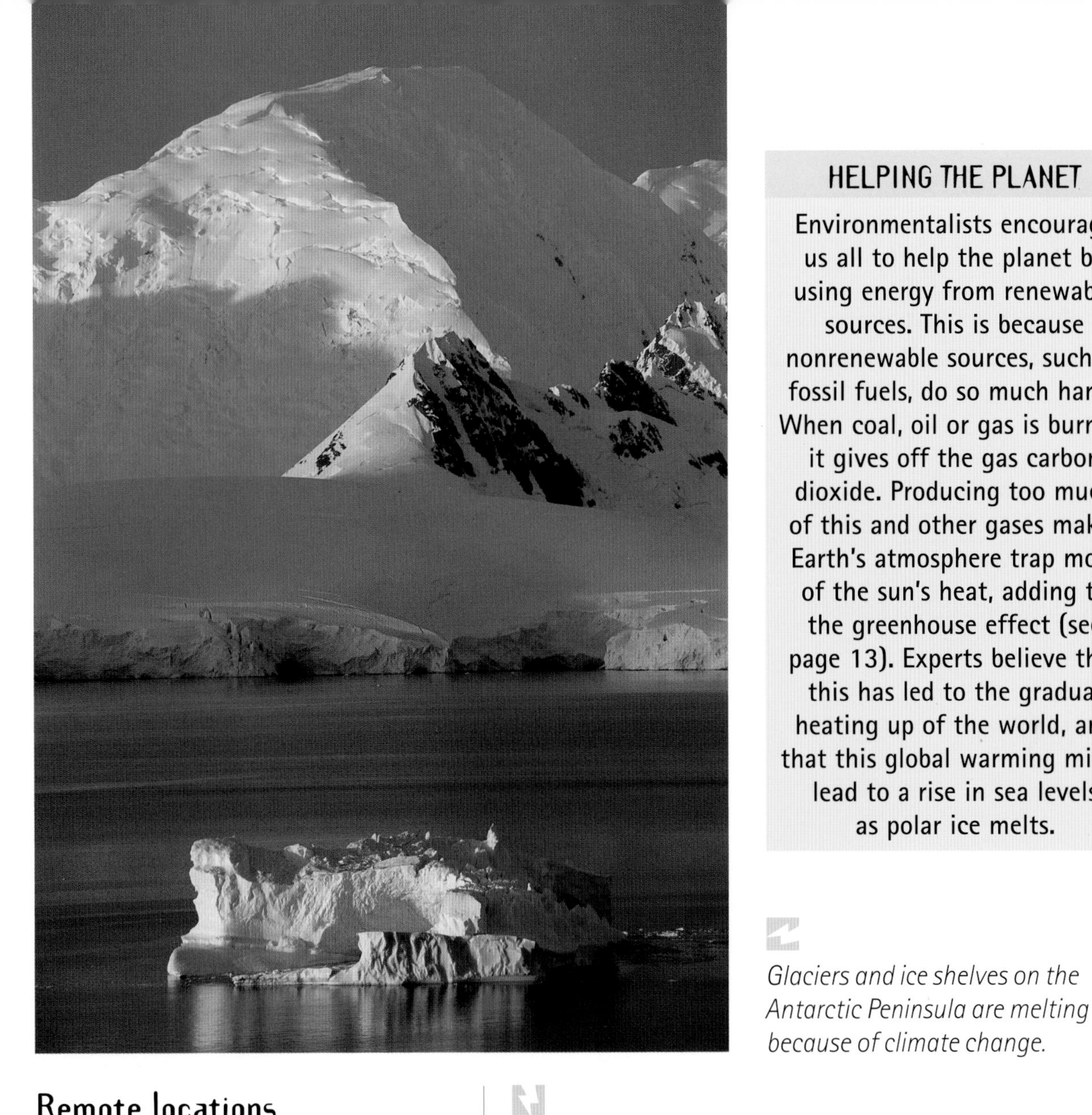

HELPING THE PLANET

Environmentalists encourage us all to help the planet by using energy from renewable sources. This is because nonrenewable sources, such as fossil fuels, do so much harm. When coal, oil or gas is burned, it gives off the gas carbon dioxide. Producing too much of this and other gases makes Earth's atmosphere trap more of the sun's heat, adding to the greenhouse effect (see page 13). Experts believe that this has led to the gradual heating up of the world, and that this global warming might lead to a rise in sea levels as polar ice melts.

Glaciers and ice shelves on the Antarctic Peninsula are melting because of climate change.

Remote locations

Solar panels are not cheap to produce, but once they are set up, they need little maintenance and cost nothing to run. This makes them very useful in parts of the world where electricity is not generally available. A good example is the southern African country of Namibia, where few people are connected to the national electricity supply. A German company runs a fleet of mobile solar-powered units, which supplies electricity to small settlements many miles from any town.

A solar-powered water pump in Namibia.

Potential problems

One of the biggest problems with solar technology is that sunlight is not constant. The amount of sunshine in any particular place changes with the seasons and individual climate conditions.

BLOT ON THE LANDSCAPE?

One of the problems with solar furnaces or towers, or powerful solar plants, is that they take up a great deal of space. They need to be well away from towns or small settlements, and deserts seem to be the ideal location. Large arrays of solar panels or reflectors spoil the look of the landscape, and many people prefer not to see them. However, other power plants are just as ugly and produce far more pollution. Solar panels for individual use are usually built into roofs and do not look unsightly.

Many people would not welcome large groups of solar panels like these near their homes.

One day there might be 10 hours of sunshine, and the next none. At night, there is certainly no sunshine. However, these problems can be overcome. The best method is to use rechargeable batteries to store solar-produced electricity. Another way is to back up a solar system with another energy source, which can be switched on if there is not enough sunshine for a particular purpose. In India and other countries, companies are building power stations that combine powerful reflectors and solar furnaces with plants fired by fossil fuels.

Cloudy conditions

Photovoltaic cells and solar panels work on dull, cloudy days, but not nearly as well as on sunny days. Some parts of the world, such as the African country of Sudan and the state of Arizona, have an average of more than 11 hours of sunshine a day. Some regions of Australia and southern Europe have more than nine hours. These are all excellent locations for solar technology. Much of Britain and Sweden, however, have less than five sunshine hours. This makes solar technology less effective.

This weather station in northern Britain is powered by the sun. It generally records up to 1,500 sunshine hours every year.

Future trends

Renewable energy sources will become more and more important in the future, as the world's demand for energy and electricity continues to increase. According to forecasts, demand for electricity will nearly double over the next 25 years.

Yet solar power still forms a tiny percentage of total energy use. It will never be able to meet huge increases in demand, unless new ways are found to harness solar energy. One way of doing this would be to send special satellites, called powersats, into space. They would have huge panels to catch solar energy and send it to Earth, perhaps along laser beams or microwaves. Whatever scientists discover and invent in the future, we should all aim to use our planet's energy more wisely and sparingly.

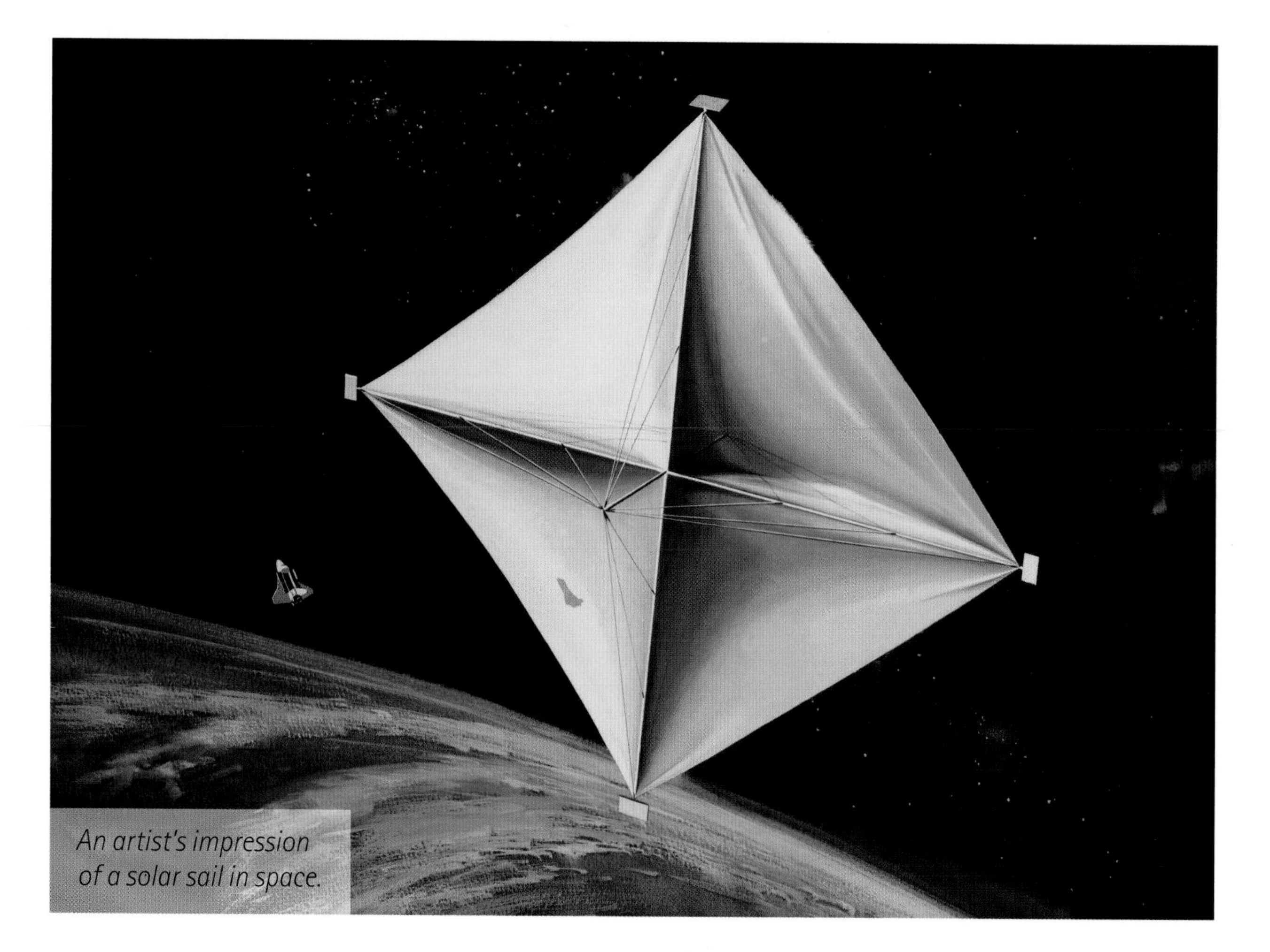

An artist's impression of a solar sail in space.

Solar sail

In June 2005, scientists launched an unmanned spacecraft called *Cosmos-1*, powered by a solar sail. This is made up of a series of giant sails that open when the spacecraft is in orbit. They catch sunlight in the same way as a ship's sails catch the wind and are pushed along by particles of solar energy known as photons. The sails are made of a very light, reflective material. However, the rocket used to launch the spacecraft failed at an early stage, and *Cosmos-1* was lost. Despite this setback, there are plans to develop the technology further.

Different forms of renewable energy may be combined to increase their power.

NEW INVENTIONS

Scientists, engineers, and inventors will continue to discover new ways to use solar power. In 2004, a group of scientists announced that they had invented a plastic solar cell that captures the sun's invisible infrared rays. This means that the cell works just as well on a cloudy day. And not only that—the plastic cell substance can be sprayed onto other materials. This means that you could spray your shirt so that it powers a mobile phone, for example. One day—perhaps not too far in the future—such inventions could change the world's use of energy.

Glossary

axis An imaginary straight line around which something spins.

chlorophyll A green chemical in plants that absorbs sunlight.

conservatory A room with a glass roof and walls.

eco-friendly Not harmful to the environment.

electromagnetic radiation The sun's rays and waves of energy, including infrared heat waves and visible light waves, made up of electric and magnetic fields.

electron A particle that occurs in atoms, circling the nucleus.

environmentalist A person who is concerned about and acts to protect the natural environment.

equator An imaginary line around the middle of Earth or another planet.

flat-bed, flat-plate, or solar collector A kind of solar panel that is used to heat water or air.

fossil fuel A fuel (such as coal, oil, or natural gas) that comes from the remains of prehistoric plants and animals.

generator A machine that turns mechanical energy into electrical energy.

global warming The rise in the temperature of Earth's surface, especially caused by pollution from burning fossil fuels.

greenhouse effect The warming of Earth's surface by the blanket of gases in the atmosphere. The effect is increased by the polluting gases released when we burn fossil fuels.

heat exchanger A device that transfers heat from one substance to another.

heliostat A movable mirror that reflects sunlight.

infrared waves Waves that lie in the range of the sun's electromagnetic radiation between visible light and radio waves.

national grid A country's network of electric power lines.

nuclear fusion The joining together of atomic nuclei.

nucleus (plural **nuclei**) The central part of an atom.

pharaoh An ancient Egyptian ruler.

photon A particle of electromagnetic radiation.

photosphere The sun's outer layer of gas.

photosynthesis The process plants use to make their own food from carbon dioxide, sunlight, and water.

photovoltaic cell A solar cell.

power station A plant where electricity is generated.

PV Short for photovoltaic.

radiation The giving off of high-energy particles such as electromagnetic waves; or energy transmitted in this way.

radio wave A kind of electromagnetic wave that can be used for long-distance communication.

rover A small vehicle that is used to explore the surface of a planet.

solar cell A small device that produces electricity directly from sunlight.

solar chimney, solar tower A tall tower in which warm air turns wind turbines to generate electricity.

solar flare A flash of radiation from the sun's surface.

solar furnace A power plant where mirrors reflect sunlight onto a fluid to heat it to a high temperature.

turbine A machine with rotating blades.

visible light The range of the sun's rays that is seen by the human eye as light.

x-ray An electromagnetic wave that can pass through materials that light cannot pass through.

Index